ACCEPTANCE

Acceptance

PAUL CHENEOUR

Redgoldmusic.com

Contents

Dedication vi

Acceptance 1

About The Author 21

To all those on the path

Copyright © 2023 by Paul Cheneour

All rights reserved. No part of this book may be reproduced in any manner whatsoever without written permission except in the case of brief quotations embodied in critical articles and reviews.

First Printing, 2023

Acceptance

After doing anything
Be sure to rest
Why run so fast
Step off the drudgery treadmill
Observe the incomparable beauty
We are only here for a moment
The end will arrive soon enough
And quicker than you expected

Be sensitive to your life
Go outside
Go into nature
Feel the wind brushing your skin
Feel the warmth of the sun
Feel the rain giving nourishment
Know when to start an adventure
Know when to hold back
Do not look for solutions outside
Focus within and remember
This physical body is
The last visible emanation
Of your material existence

Stay positive
Even in the face of adversity
This day could be the last
Taste the succulent flavour
In every morsel of life
Smell the delicious scents
Savour each beautiful moment
As it arrives and departs

Allow yourself to be loved
Do not close your mind
Do not close your heart
Do not create a prison
Without bars
Open your chest
Let the spirits move in and out
Glow with your love giving
Allow yourself to be loved

Accept that you are perfectly imperfect
Especially through difficult times
Look beyond your limitations
To the field out beyond the idea
Of wrong doing or right doing
Where separation does not exist
Be gentle with your imperfections
They are there to serve and remind you
Of the wonderous path you have taken
Towards yourself
Be grateful for this beautiful gift

Turn sufferings
Into wisdom
Choose differently
A second time

Drink
Only
From the
Fountain
Of light

From bewilderment
To wonderment
To whom
Does this truth belong to
Anyway

All answers
Arrive
In
Silence

This now moment
Is but a moment in time
Savour the flavour
Of its deliciousness

Be in peace
As you weave your own
Blissful story
I can see you now
Please know
That I am here too

What do I carry
With me on this road
My essence
What do I leave behind
Unnecessary baggage

The looking glass reflection
Shows a faint image
Learn who you really are
Stumbling and falling
Precariously
Until one day
You stand upright

We live in strange times
Have courage to face
The dark night of the soul
Stand on the edge of the abyss
Ready to cross into the unknown
Remember humans do not think
In straight lines

Stop making judgements about
Weaponised consumerism
Market forces
Corporatism
Or any other ism
See with open eyes
Be serene
Within this clarity
A new vision will arise

A new route magically opens
Be gently pointed in the
Direction towards yourself
Listen to your inner voice
Ask to be shown what you need
Rather than what you think you want

Music
Magic
Mystery
Are what we are given
Do not let the robbers steal them
They are your precious gifts
And sacred birth rights

Knife and fork
Separated
By a plate
Working together
Through human hands
One meeting
One Chance
Ichi-go-ichi-e

Functionless metaphors
Fill the air
In sober silence

Rabid snivelling man toady
Is just a fading memory
Consigned to the dark ages
Of that dog eat dog paradigm

What happened
At the break of day
Where did that time go
Is this really the end
Why did events
Happen like that
Did we manage to
Turn from grey
To green

Time lines will converge soon
Whatever choices we made
Will have no effect
We will see with new eyes
The old game is over
Checkmate
A human upgrade
Is taking place
There are no more hiding places
Surrender to this inevitability
And bathe in glorious blissfulness

A Crow on the quarry ledge
Screeches out
A loud sarcastic squawk saying
I told you so
But do we humans ever listen

It is time to go home
Ready or not
Be content
With all you have done
You did what you could
With what you had
So feel contented

An inner suppressed rage is
Demanding to be heard
Keeping it hidden makes it stronger
Trust your intuition to find the key
When you unlock that soul door
Rage will finally dissolve into peace

Walk with Me
Beyond hope and hopelessness
Intellectualism and Emotionalism
All your wants and needs
Are being met in the Tao
Through the trial of tears
You are on the long walk home
And now an Adept
On the path of least resistance
Is this liberation
Yes
No
Perhaps

Give up fighting
You chose to be here
In this physical form
With all its limitations
But you feel small and insignificant
When you find true understanding
And the commitments you made
You will realise how gigantic you are

Words are vibration spells
Together with thoughts and intention
They have an enormous power
Be positive in everything
You say and do

Come one come all
Gather round this fire fest
Bathe in the glowing embers
Of eternal love and warmth

In the night air
Darting and crackling
Succulent souls are waking
From their deepest slumbers
Ready to unfold furled wings
And fly into skies of imagination

Obedience
Depends on lies
Misdirection
And more lies

Unlearn the head stuffing
Of formal education
Look within yourself
Discover your best teacher

A Professor cleverly says
Time emerges from activity
The law of cause and effect
Is yet to be fully understood
By the material reality world mindset
This virus arrived from maladministration
It is time to see ourselves for what we are
And to appreciate what we could become
The time has come the walrus said
Oh dear
Said Piglet

The real pandemic
We should be addressing
Is poverty
In all its debilitating forms

Slowdown and be still
Quieten the internal noise
Focus attention inward
Taste each morsel
Placed in your mouth
Savour the minutest textures
Show gratitude for this gift
Of sustenance

Sanckbard the fierce sat
Pompously pontificating
Oozing righteous indignation
Over some official slight
No one listened then
He began thumping his fists
Harder and harder
Until bones began cracking
Snackbardetta the present
Sat motionless
Studiously ignoring his plight
There will be a day of reckoning
You can be sure of that he said

Things are as they are
Even if they seem incongruent
And out of kilter
In complete chaos
There is an order
Only a few can perceive
Sit still and observe
All will become apparent
In due course
You will see

Slip sliding
Down the hill
Of predictability
Towards uncertainty

Each day brings new possibilities
With opportunities to change
To be different
To be greater than yesterday
Open that door
In your perception
That invites in new thinking

You arrived glowing
Full with radiance
As you grew
Your light dimmed
To a mere flicker
Reignite your flame
And shine brightly
Be luminescent
Like the star
You are meant to be

Subtle scents of autumn are approaching
New cocktails of olfactory delights
Wait cautiously in the wings
As we lay to rest lustful
Summer fragrances

It is time
To look past the veil
To see what is
And what is
Not real
In your world

Do not be seduced
Or flattered by
The silky tongues
Of the enslavers
Sharpen your instincts
For smelling
Odorous falsities

Language constantly evolves
With changes twists and turns
Understood only in hindsight
There is a new trend happening
That hides behind
Noncommittal nothing speak
With empty words
Devoid of feeling
Devoid of sense
Devoid of loving
Designed to pacify
To prohibit questioning
Or useful understanding
Time for another change
In the language direction

Punctuality
Is a mark of respect
To yourself
To friendships
To lovers
To your beloved

Anxiety prevents enlightenment
When you hear a lullaby
Soul leaves the body and
Enters the world of imagination
Be energised
And dance with delirious passion

Take the lead
Do not wait to react
Be bold
Be adventurous
Give yourself permission
To be glorious

The enslaver uses
Humiliation
Intimidation
And blackmail
Stand tall and solid
Refuse to submit
To any abuse
Discover your own
True strength

Stinkweed the unpleasant
Does not give a tinkers cuss
About who he offends
Annoys or upsets
He oozes contempt for anyone
Daring to question
His right to be obnoxious
There he sits alone and oblivious in a
Smouldering stench of his own making

Multitudes of thoughts
Feelings and
Emotions
Move outwards
Faster than light
Daring to be caught
In the language net
Just a few are slow enough
To be impaled and become a
Precis of a human being

As a newcomer to this absurdity
You may hear some loud bangs
And unavoidable silences
The seaweed trifle sits alone
Lemon concrete hardens
While tapioca fudge laughs at
Thrice smited seasoning
Limping snow shoes
Surf the sand dunes
Of the rational mind
You do know all this makes sense

For whom does the willow weep
It weeps for thee
And for me
Casting its long shadow
Over fading memories
From the light of the sun
On this raggedy
Scurrying
Fragment of a
Human being

Glymtosh
Slimetoad
Salivate
Grenfick
Aloysius
Ponte and
Bob
Are no longer
Taking telepathic calls
From unevolved beings

Watch your language
Words have weight and power
Beyond your knowing
Do not listen to the daily travail
In this dismal land
Of sadness and doom
Speak well
Be sure your words
Resonate with love
Kindness and compassion

When one of us crosses the divide
Be inspired to love more deeply
Put aside your squabbling
And grubbing in the dirt of desire
For gold
For treasure
For prestige
For power
Be moved to love more deeply
The weight of your life
Will be blessed and weighed
More than you can imagine

Are we there yet
I hear you ask
Before this journey ends
There are seven valleys to cross
Where are they
I hear you ask again
No one knows
No messenger has returned to tell the tale
First is the valley of the quest
Then the wide valley of love
The next is of insight to mystery
Followed by detachment and serenity
After that lies the valley of unity
Leading to awe and deep bewilderment
The seventh is poverty and nothingness
Where you are suspended motionless
Until as a drop you are absorbed into
A sea with no shorelines
Are we there yet
You may well ask

Why is wisdom measured in pearls

Why seek validation
From deductive reasoning
From an insane system
Designed to destroy you
When all that is needed
Is to be tested against
Experience and truth

A two inch steel nail sits poised
Waiting in fevered anticipation
For the delicious kiss of the hammer
Driving it to its fulfilment
In life
Be both nail and hammer
Be thankful for trials and tribulations
Driving you forward
Towards complete fulfilment

In this time of sensory smog
And information overload
Refuse to be seduced
By defeatism
Do not give in to idle stagnation
Your loan voice however faint
Has permission to be heard
You also have permission to be seen
You are more significant than you know
Be wild and plant seeds of knowing
Watch ideas sprout wings
Listen to thoughts ripen
Into actions of clarity
The smog is perceptibly lifting

Down by the glistening shoreline
The image collector studiously
Rummages through past memories
A time line opens
In this gully of curious obsessions
Tread wisely
Tread carefully
Thieves and bandits
Lie in wait to snare and
Tear your passions from you

How should I describe my pain
Who will hear my beleaguered cry
What is the point of these words
Carried by wind over land and sea
To hide in desert crevasses for aeons
Take that one small step
On the way
On the path
If you do hear these words however softly
That alone is my reward

Standing on this threshold
Panning for signs of life
New ideas arrive squeezed
Like lemons juiced
Murmuring water tickles my ear
Words tumble from my pen
Filling the uncharted page
Now I am sighing with relief
At last something coherent
Is making
An appearance

Sipping sunlight
Through glass straws
Stumbling like a drunkard
Shaky with unsure footing
Arms flailing everywhere
Resist all and any coercion
Stand firm in Self knowing
Be the rock in the stream
Washed and rounded by water
Let every fibre of your being
Unravel

Night comes
A chance to dream
Listen to what soul
Is sharing with you
In your own language

Dusk descends kissing the ground
Any separation between you and I
Is gone forever
When we lay down together
In that meadow of unity
The idea of each other
Makes no sense
We are in each other
In complete completeness

In the beginning
A loud bang was heard
Loud enough to wake the dead
While the waiter was serving
Seaweed trifle
Lemon concrete
Tapioca fudge cake
Topped off with
Absurd seasoning
The ending is getting ever closer

In Between yes and no
Lost in Bewilderment
More than can be measured
With a foot in both worlds
Finding a bridge
Would end this despair
Do not try to understand this fate
Say farewell to all you have known
Turn towards the delight
Of not knowing
And fly free

Enter an obscure oblivion
In the valley of poverty and nothingness
Having weathered every test on the path
And being lost in this unknown place
You have grown wise in the quest
Go peacefully now
Towards the realms of delight
Liberation is knocking at your door
Flames burn illusions to the core
The truth we seek
The name of which we cannot speak
Is finally revealed
When all identity disappears

Just like dust particles
Dancing in sunlight rays
Streaming through a window
We bob and gyrate
To the sound of an
Unseen orchestra
Where you and I
Are just flecks
Of possibilities

There is a constant thought
That at any moment
Everything you trust
Will be taken from you
It is in your conditioning
Facing this fear
Takes enormous courage
Live peacefully in peace
And in
Acceptance
Of all
That
You are

Paul Cheneour has walked a broader musical path throughout his career embracing European Classical, Jazz, Arab, Indian, Celtic, and other music's, culminating in his own 'World Fusion' style.

"Tapping into the source of creativity takes great courage and even greater competence in acquired skills.
Paul Cheneour, a leading UK jazz, classical and ethnic flautist/composer suffered a near fatal car crash in '91.

He recovered with the conviction that he needed to use his talent, life, and near-death experience to explore a new forms of creative expression. This amounts to an opening out to the influences available in the moment.

All the world's great musical and artistic traditions remain as resources and are no longer seen as restrictive boundaries"

(Interview extract by Michael Greevis for Colour Therapy Magazine UK. 1995)

www.ingramcontent.com/pod-product-compliance
Lightning Source LLC
Chambersburg PA
CBHW021135080526
44587CB00012B/1299